Center for
Creative
Leadership

Learning Tactics Inventory

FACILITATOR'S GUIDE

Maxine Dalton, PhD

Published by CCL Press

Author
Maxine Dalton, PhD

With Special Thanks
Dawn Barts, John Fleenor, Shaun Martin, Stephen Rush, Peter Scisco, Sylvester Taylor

Director of Assessments, Tools, and Publications
Sylvester Taylor

Manager, Publication Development
Peter Scisco

Editor
Stephen Rush

Associate Editor
Shaun Martin

Design and Layout
Diana Coe

Rights and Permissions
Kelly Lombardino

Editorial Board
David Altman, Elaine Biech, Regina Eckert, Joan Gurvis, Jennifer Habig, Kevin Liu, Neal Maillet, Jennifer Martineau, Portia Mount, Laura Santana

CCL. No. 8016
ISBN No. 978-1-60491-549-5

CENTER FOR CREATIVE LEADERSHIP
WWW.CCL.ORG

Contents

Acknowledgments

I WOULD LIKE TO THANK THE STAFF at the Army Research Institute at Ft. Leavenworth, Kansas, especially Dr. Stan Halpin, Dr. Joan Silver, and Kathy Fuegen, for their invaluable assistance on this project. I would also like to thank Diane Young at the Center for Creative Leadership and Dr. Leo Burke and Motorola University for providing data-collection opportunities. I thank Edna Parrott, Denise Craig, Mary White, and Patti Hall at the Center for Creative Leadership for their careful attention to data entry and preparation of the manuscript and my colleagues, Amy Webb, Ellen Van Velsor, Kerry Bunker, and Jill Waccholz, for the time spent talking through the topic, reading manuscripts, and advising me on aspects of this project. My research colleague, Silvia Swigert, has provided insight, expertise, and invaluable assistance in the development of the instrument. Craig Chappelow, Michael Wakefield, Winn Legerton, and other CCL program managers and trainers, as well as the participants in CCL programs, have provided data-collection opportunities. Finally, I would like to thank Amy Webb, Michael Lombardo, and Kerry Bunker for first teaching me about learning to learn.

Introduction

THERE IS A WIDESPREAD CONSENSUS THAT PEOPLE learn critical management and leadership skills from the naturally occurring experiences of the workplace—from challenging assignments, coaches, role models, and even hardships. However, all individuals do not learn equally well from these experiences, and some individuals even resist or avoid unfamiliar opportunities for learning.

The *Learning Tactics Inventory* (LTI) is designed for individuals who wish to become better at learning from experience. The LTI provides these individuals with information about how they learn and illustrates behaviors that they can adopt to become more versatile learners.

The learning behaviors that an individual employs when mastering the challenge of an unfamiliar work assignment are undoubtedly related to that person's personality and style of processing information. The LTI does not attempt to measure personality or information-processing style, but rather offers an inventory of the behaviors that individuals have reported using when engaged in the task of learning from experience. The premise of the LTI is that individuals can improve their ability to learn from experience if they first develop an awareness of how they learn and then, subsequently, expand their repertoire of learning behaviors.

Learning Tactics Inventory Facilitator's Guide Package

The Learning Tactics Inventory Facilitator's Guide package consists of the following components:

- This *Learning Tactics Inventory Self-Assessment Survey*
- The *Learning Tactics Inventory Participant Workbook*
- The *Learning Tactics Inventory Facilitator's Guide*

The *Learning Tactics Inventory Self-Assessment Survey* provides a set of scores that can be compared to the aggregate scores of a reference group (norms) to illustrate how an individual reports learning when faced with a novel or unfamiliar challenge. These results can assist individuals who fill out the survey to understand how they learn and how these behavior patterns influence where and what they learn or fail to learn. This process of becoming aware is called meta-cognition and means "paying attention to the process of learning." It is a first step in becoming a more versatile learner.

The Learning Tactics Inventory Participant Workbook is provided to help individuals understand their LTI scores, thereby enabling them to do the following:

- Identify their preferred learning patterns;
- Identify tactics they avoid using;
- Recognize how their patterns may cause them to misuse or avoid particular work-based challenges;

- Adopt new learning behaviors; and
- Begin to set learning goals rather than performance goals.

The *Learning Tactics Inventory Facilitator's Guide* helps facilitators, trainers, and presenters by providing:
- An explanation of the underlying learning model;
- Suggestions for presenting the model to others;
- A description of applications and uses for the LTI;
- A sample workshop design and administrative suggestions;
- The underlying theory and research related to the instrument's reliability and validity;
- Suggested resources; and
- Powerpoint slides.

Questions Addressed

The LTI addresses two questions associated with the practice of learning managerial and leadership skills from experience:
- Why do some people learn from the opportunities of the workplace, while others fail to do so?
- Can individuals improve their ability to learn from experience?

Our research and practice have led us to believe that some people fail to learn from the challenges of the workplace, either because they avoid the opportunity altogether or because they use inappropriate learning tactics. They do what is comfortable rather than what is most appropriate or effective. We believe that individuals can improve their ability to learn from experience if they will take the time to understand their learning habits or preferences and then consciously expand them.

Explanation

The *Learning Tactics Inventory* (LTI) was developed to provide individuals with a concrete representation of the tactics they most frequently use when they are challenged to learn from a new situation. Other instruments that measure characteristics of learning, such as Kolb's (1984) *Learning Styles Inventory*, Wagner and Sternberg's (1991) *Tacit Knowledge Inventory*, or the *Myers-Briggs Type Inventory* (Myers & McCaulley, 1988), measure learning style from the inside out, conceptualizing preferred methods of learning as trait-based or as information-processing strategies. The *Learning Tactics Inventory* depicts learning from the outside in as a set of behavioral tactics that an individual employs to engage in and learn from a challenging opportunity (Curry, 1987).

The *Learning Tactics Inventory* is designed to show individuals the tactics they use most and the tactics they use least so that they can then consciously decide to become more flexible learners by adopting tactics that are not part of their current behavioral repertoires.

The LTI is intended for use during the process of developmental planning when the developmental strategy is to engage in challenging and unfamiliar work assignments. Individuals who intend to participate in challenging situations in order to learn new skills can use information from the *Learning Tactics Inventory* to identify how they learn. They can then incorporate new tactics into their developmental plans.

What the *Learning Tactics Inventory* Measures

The LTI measures four kinds of learning tactics—behaviors identified in the research literature as characteristic learning strategies. Figure 1 lists some of the sample items. The four sets of learning tactics are labeled *Action* (learning from direct experience), *Thinking* (learning through symbolic representation), *Feeling* (learning by managing the anxiety that would otherwise interfere with engaging in the challenging situation), and *Accessing Others* (socially transmitted learning).

Action

The items that represent *Action* tactics are drawn from the work of Revans (1980) and Bandura (1977). They are characteristic of learning that occurs from performing actions and experiencing the effects. When individuals use *Action* learning tactics, they engage in the task at hand, learning from the situation itself and not necessarily waiting for all of the data or the responses of others.

Thinking

The items that represent *Thinking* tactics are drawn from the work of Meichenbaum, Price, Phares,

Action	Briefly sketch what I think needs to be done and do it. Immerse myself in the situation so that I can learn quickly.
Thinking	Mentally rehearse my actions before going into the situation. Picture myself doing well.
Feeling	Trust my feelings about what to do. Acknowledge the impact of my feelings on what I decide to do.
Accessing Others	Talk to someone who has had the same experience. Emulate the behavior of another person.

Figure 1. Sample Items on the LTI by Category

McCormick, and Hyde (1989) and Bandura (1977). *Thinking* tactics describe those behaviors that are solitary and internal, including (1) reflecting on the past to draw parallels, contrasts, and rules of thumb and (2) anticipating the future through cognitive rehearsal and if/then possibilities. *Thinking* tactics represent both metaphorical inductive strategies and hypothesis-generating deductive strategies (Mezirow, 1990).

Bandura describes *Thinking* tactics as symbolic experience—a way to process and preserve experience to serve as a guide to future behavior, to project images of a desirable future, and to solve problems by considering alternative solutions and outcomes.

Feeling

The items that represent *Feeling* tactics are drawn from the work of Kolb (1984) and Horney (1970). These items represent those behaviors that individuals employ to acknowledge and manage the feelings of anxiety or discomfort that arise from facing an unknown challenge. Individuals cannot learn from experience if they are not willing to first engage in the experience. Additionally, they must recognize feelings of psychological discomfort that might cause them to engage the experience in the most comfortable/habitual way, rather than in the most effective way.

Accessing Others

These items represent observational and vicarious behaviors—modeling and seeking advice, support, counsel, coaching, or formal training from others. They are drawn from the work of Bandura (1977).

The premise behind the *Learning Tactics Inventory* is that how people learn and what they learn are inextricably bound. It is assumed that individuals who have a greater variety of learning tactics at their disposal are more likely to approach and learn from a greater variety of situations. For example, individuals who typically learn by reading "how to" books would presumably find it difficult to develop their interpersonal skills solely by reading books about how to get along with others. They would also need to use *Feeling* tactics to manage any anxiety they might have about approaching others and *Accessing Others* tactics to model and practice the desired interpersonal behaviors and receive feedback about their efforts. Figure 2 provides a chart illustrating the negative consequences of using one set of tactics to the exclusion of the others.

	Action Without	Thinking Without	Feeling Without	Accessing Others Without
Action		Procrastination.	Paralysis.	Talk the issue to death.
Thinking	May not have the vital information. May not extract all the learning from the consequences of action. May repeat actions not successful in the past.		Overrespond to emotional aspects without the calming influence of reason/past success.	Lose the information that resides within formal sources or within one's self.
Feeling	Ignore/deny feelings and slip into habitual responses.	Intellectualize, rationalize to avoid the task.		Misuse others to avoid the task.
Accessing Others	Reinvent the wheel, no support, may offend.	Miss the knowledge and support of others. The benefit of others to push, challenge one's thinking.	Unnecessary isolation.	

Figure 2. Consequences of Overuse of Learning Tactics

Applications

THE LTI IS DESIGNED TO BE USED FOR CAREER OR MANAGEMENT development by individuals and their managers, or by trainers, HRD professionals, or personal coaches when the goal is to help individuals become more versatile learners. More specifically, the tool may be used to introduce individuals to the following:

The Concept of Learning Management and Leadership Skills from Work-Based Experiences. For many individuals career development and management development are event-based and translate into "taking a course," "watching a video," or "reading a book." In fact, research in the past two decades underscores that the majority of management and leadership skills are learned from naturally occurring experiences in the workplace.

The Concept of Meta-Cognition, or Paying Attention to How One Learns. Many individuals have never thought about how they learn, and yet educators have demonstrated the importance of this awareness for improving the ability to learn. The LTI introduces a language and a framework that allow individuals to begin to think about how they learn.

The Importance of Setting Learning Goals That Correspond with Task-Based Performance Goals. Many individuals think about personal development as something they will do when they have time—after the work is done. Consequently, annual developmental goals are rarely attended to, or accomplished, as individuals are too busy doing the work. The LTI is one strategy for helping individuals understand that personal developmental goals can be accomplished as a part of the work, that is, the developmental opportunity is imbedded in the real work of the organization.

The Importance of Seeking Out and Engaging in Novel and Unfamiliar Work-Based Challenges. Many individuals limit their career growth by avoiding tasks that they do not already know how to do or feel they might not do well. Mastery of these tasks, however, is essential to personal growth, and individuals need to recognize the importance of seeking out a broad variety of managerial and leadership challenges.

Strategies and Tactics for Managing the Anxiety Associated with "Not Knowing." Individuals need concrete behavioral strategies for managing the anxiety associated with novel work in order that they do not avoid the task or engage the task using unproductive but familiar learning tactics.

The Relationship Between How we Learn and What we Learn. Often, the things individuals are not good at doing are inextricably linked with how they learn. The LTI is designed to illustrate to individuals that learning certain skills may require the use of new tactics. For example, to become more interpersonally skilled may require the use of *Accessing Others* tactics; to learn decisiveness may require the use of *Action* tactics; to learn to become more thorough may require the use of *Thinking* tactics; and to engage in any unfamiliar task may require the use of *Feeling* tactics.

Administration of the LTI

> The LTI is not a measure of personality or information-processing style. It is not meant to be used to label individuals nor to suggest immutable trait-based abilities or motivational preferences. Use of this survey for any purpose other than to increase self-awareness for personal development is a misuse of the tool.

THE LTI SHOULD BE ADMINISTERED PRIOR TO ANY EXPLANATION or discussion of the four tactics: *Action, Thinking, Feeling,* and *Accessing Others.*

The inventory consists of thirty-two questions and requires approximately 15 minutes to complete. For each item there are five possible response choices, ranging from "I have almost never used this approach" to "I have almost always used this approach." Respondents are asked to think about the times in their lives when they have been faced with the challenge of an unfamiliar task or experience. After reading each item, they are to indicate the extent to which each of the learning approaches has been characteristic of their behavior.

The LTI is self-scoring. The answer sheet is filled out across the rows from left to right, and the scores for each category are computed by adding the eight scores in each column. Scores should then be graphed on the bar graph on page 9 of the participant workbook.

Presentation Design

The following is a suggested sequence for using the LTI as part of a group presentation. Individuals who wish to use the LTI on their own or managers who wish to use the LTI with individuals can easily extrapolate the learning points from this outline.

It is anticipated that trainers will develop their own presentations. This material is offered as a sample or template for a delivery module. The slides can be found in the section titled "Presentation Slides" at the end of this guide.

Step 1: Introduce the Concept of Learning from Experience (3 minutes)

SLIDE 1	A majority of the managerial and leadership skills that individuals report as critical to their careers were learned from the naturally occurring experiences of the workplace. (See McCall, Lombardo, & Morrison, 1988.)

SLIDE 2	Think of your entire career up to this point. Jot down some of the key events that have made a difference in your career, things that led to a lasting change in how you manage. Choose one of these events to share with your small group, giving the following information:
	
	    What happened?
	    What did you learn from this event (for better or worse)?

Step 2: Design a Presentation from the Following Information (10–15 minutes)

	Research first conducted at the Center for Creative Leadership in the mid-1980s and replicated many times since has demonstrated that successful individuals report learning many of the skills that make them effective as managers and leaders from the work itself—from challenging assignments, from good and bad bosses, mentors, colleagues, and coaches, and even from hardships. In fact, about 75 percent of the events that individuals report as critical to their careers come from a combination of learning from the work itself and learning from others. Individuals who aspire to higher level managerial roles within an organization must think about their careers not only as mastery of professional, technical, or functional skills but also as mastery of the challenges taught by a variety of managerial tasks. For example, managing a start-up teaches one set of lessons, whereas managing a downsizing or a turnaround teaches another. The effective manager masters the lessons taught by a variety of challenging experiences. He or she does not become locked into one way to behave.
SLIDE 3	After each group member has identified at least three critical events and shared at least one of them with the others in his or her small group, use Slide 3 as an outline for discussion. The slide illustrates the results of the CCL research. Define what each category means, using experiences drawn from the organization that the participants are familiar with as examples. Ask them to think about how many of these challenges they have had in their own careers. What would the holes be in their resumes if they were to list managerial challenges instead of functional assignments to illustrate their career progress? For more information see the suggested resources section.

Step 3: Distribute a Participant Workbook (12–15 minutes)

	After giving everyone a copy of the workbook, instruct participants to complete the inventory on pages 1 and 2. Tell them that they will have about 15 minutes.

Step 4: Assign Reading (5–10 minutes)

	After everyone has completed the survey, instruct the participants to read the sections titled "Background" and "Four Sets of Learning Behaviors" in their workbooks.

Step 5: Give a Presentation (25–30 minutes)

	Give the following presentation and then discuss what you have said with the group.

As we have discussed, experience teaches critical management and leadership skills. So who learns and who does not learn from experience? It has been shown that individuals who are most successful at learning from experience use the greatest variety of learning tactics. Becoming a versatile learner is not easy; it requires going against the grain of how one prefers to learn.

In 1989 and 1990 Mike Lombardo, Kerry Bunker, and Amy Webb of the Center for Creative Leadership conducted a study on the topic of learning how to learn. They wanted to understand who is most able to learn from experience and under what conditions. They observed a group of high-potential individuals to see if and how they were able to accomplish their individual developmental goals over the course of one year. They had information about the personality and learning history of these individuals; the learning history described the learning tactics the participants reported using over the course of their lives. These learning tactics fell into four major categories: *Action, Thinking, Feeling*, and *Accessing Others*.

The researchers found that individuals differed in their ability and willingness to learn from experience. The individuals who were most successful in achieving their developmental goals were those who used the greatest variety of learning tactics. Individuals who were less successful in attaining their goals were more cautious and reactive in their approach to learning and employed fewer learning tactics. Individuals who were never able to achieve their goals were those who avoided the task or who used only a few tactics, often trying the same thing over and over, whether it was working or not.

Individuals who were able to improve their ability to learn from experience were able to expand the number and variety of learning tactics that they used. Learning to learn involved meta-cognition—paying attention to how they liked to learn—and going against what was familiar or comfortable to use other learning tactics.

Research conducted in the mid-1990s by Maxine Dalton and Silvia Swigert has confirmed the relationship between using all four tactics and being perceived as a more effective learner.

SLIDE 4	Slide 4 depicts the four tactics that are related to effective learning. When individuals are faced with the opportunity to engage in a challenging task, they must first decide whether they are going to accept the challenge. They must use *Feeling* tactics to manage the anxiety of the unknown and accept the challenge. As they do so, and because they are striving to become more versatile learners, they will then be able to choose the tactics or sequence of tactics that makes the most sense given the task. They cannot simply do what is comfortable, but must face the challenge and engage the task in the most appropriate way.

Step 6: Graph the Results (10 minutes)

	Next, direct the participants to transfer their scores from the LTI to the Scoring Sheet on page 7 of their workbooks and then to graph their results on the bar graph on page 8.

Step 7: Integrate the Data (3 minutes per group member)

	What a person needs to know and how he or she learns it are connected. Ask participants to note all of the tactics that they rated 1 or 2 and note these on page 10. Ask them to determine whether all of the tactics they rated in this way fall into one category or whether they are scattered across the four sets of tactics. Ask them to discuss within their small groups how the tactics they have used have influenced what they have learned and where they have learned it.

Step 8: Examine Learning Tactics (3 minutes per group member)

	Remind participants that tactics can be misused or overused as well as underused. Ask individuals to note all of the tactics that they rated 4 or 5 on page 10 of their workbooks. Ask them to determine whether all of the tactics they rated in this way fall into one category or whether they are scattered across the four sets of tactics. Ask them to discuss within their small groups how the tactics they have used have influenced what they have learned and where they have learned it.

Step 9: Developmental Planning (10 minutes)

	Ask everyone to think about his or her own career goals and the skills needed to achieve those goals. After a few minutes for consideration, ask them to select one or more tactics that they will intentionally try to use from now on in order to further their own learning. Have them note on their Personal Development Plans on pages 15 and 16 of their workbooks what they will try and when and where they will try it.

Step 10: Reinforce Major Points (10 minutes)

	Remind the participants that the goal of the training is to become a more versatile learner so that they can:
	Seek out and use the opportunities that life affords;
	Learn in ways best suited to the situation; and
	Manage the anxiety associated with learning new skills using new tactics, that is, going against one's comfort level.

Step 11: Wrap Up the Session (15 minutes)

SLIDE 5	Lead a discussion of Slide 5, which illustrates what happens when an individual avoids a learning experience. Learning new things often results in an initial drop-off in performance. If an individual is afraid, he or she may return to an old way of doing things. Use analogies to explain the concept, such as trying to improve one's backhand in tennis or change one's golf grip. It feels awkward at first, but one must persist. If you give up, performance returns to its former level, but the learning opportunity is lost and there is no improvement.
SLIDE 6	Slide 6 illustrates what happens when one accepts the challenge and harvests the learning. Briefly discuss the point with the group.
SLIDE 7	Slide 7 summarizes the main points of the session: (1) finding out what you do not do well; (2) choosing projects that can serve as learning tools; and (3) trying new tactics. Discuss these with the group and gain each person's commitment to break the mold and try some new tactics to become more versatile learners.

Additional Points

If using the LTI in a classroom setting the following guidelines are offered:

1. The LTI represents a broad range of learning behaviors grouped into similar sets. No inference should be made from a score about an individual's personality, style, or character. Rather, a score is quite simply self-reported use of certain tactics: "You say you do a lot of *this* and that you hardly ever do *that*. Are there implications in this pattern that speak to what you learn, where you learn it, how you learn, and what you may fail to learn?"

2. On page 9 in the *Learning Tactics Inventory Participant Workbook* there is a bar graph for individuals to compare their own scores to a normative sample. This normative sample is 188 individuals who were participants in the Center for Creative Leadership's Leadership Development Program; the mean, standard deviation, and median scores, as well as the demographic characteristics of the sample, are described in Table 1. The bar graph allows a participant to graph his or her scores against the percentiles of the normative sample and to obtain a rough estimate of the sets of behaviors he or she uses as compared with the sample population. As a rule of thumb, individuals who report using all four tactics at a level above the 50th percentile are describing themselves as versatile learners. After looking at the overall picture, however, it is most useful for individuals to return to the items themselves and find those behaviors that they say they never use—the items on which they scored themselves as "1" or "2." These are the behaviors that they may wish to commit to try in the future to further their own learning and developmental goals.

3. Some people find that their scores fall below the 50th percentile on all four scales. This may reflect a personal response set, such as never using 5's when responding to Likert scales. Or it may reflect the failure of the instrument to capture the total range of learning behaviors. It may be that the individual has never spent time thinking about how he or she learns and that it will take some time for reflection before he or she is able to fill out the instrument in a meaningful way. This should be explained to the participants. They should be directed to find their highest and lowest scale scores and then return to the individual items to sort out their own highest and lowest item scores. Participants may also want to reflect on the learning tactics they do use if they do not think all their methods are included by this instrument.

4. The LTI is offered as a pedagogical tool to make learning behaviors concrete and, thus, easier to understand and adopt. Lombardo, Bunker, and Webb (1990) proposed that individuals who use a variety of learning tactics are better able to learn from their experiences and will, by implication, be more effective managers and leaders in the workplace. Work to further explore and demonstrate these hypotheses continues.

Means, Standard Deviation, and Median Scores for Normative Sample (N = 188)

	Action	Thinking	Feeling	Accessing Others
Mean	28.79	28.59	22.51	25.56
Standard deviation	3.41	4.30	4.70	4.23
Median	29	28	23	26

Demographic characteristics of the normative sample:

84 percent from the U.S.
75.4 percent caucasian; 3.2 percent black; 2.1 percent hispanic
76.1 percent mid-level managers; 5.9 percent individual contributors or first line supervisors;
15.5 percent senior managers
62.6 percent male; 21.4 percent female
Average age = 40.90
Average education = 17.29

When percent is less than 100 percent, information is missing.

Table 1. LTI Scores for a Normative Sample

Research

THE STEPS TAKEN IN DEVELOPING THE INSTRUMENT, how the items were developed, the internal consistency of the four scales (reliability), and the research conducted to determine the construct and concurrent validity of the instrument are described below. Research results that demonstrate the relationship of the LTI to meta-cognition and to personality as measured by the *Myers-Briggs Type Inventory*, although not conclusive, will also be presented here.

Item Generation

Items were generated through conversations with the investigators from the pilot learning study at the Center for Creative Leadership, from anecdotal journal entries during the same study, and from the literature on learning, specifically, Bandura (1977), Kolb (1984), Michenbaum et al. (1989), and Revans (1990). Nineteen items were also generated from the neo-analytic literature (Horney, 1970) describing the ability and willingness of individuals to engage in novel situations. Seventy-five items were tested with a variety of rating scales and formats.

The rating format chosen directs the respondents as follows:

> "Think about times you have been faced with the challenge of an unfamiliar task or experience. Using the scale of 1 to 5 as defined below, circle the number that best indicates the extent that each of the approaches listed has been characteristic of your behavior."

Anchor points for the scale range from (1) "I have almost never used this approach" to (5) "I have almost always used this approach." Scores on each item are summed across the eight items making up each scale. The maximum score of 40 indicates that a tactic is always used; a score of 8 indicates that a tactic is almost never used.

Reliability

Data to ascertain the internal consistency (reliability) of the scales were collected over a two-year period from participants in two courses sponsored by the Center for Creative Leadership and from a military officers training school over a one-year period. Theory and item-to-total scores were used to determine which items provided the best fit and coverage of the domains. An item-to-total score correlates an item with the total scale and indicates the degree to which each item belongs with the rest of the items on the scale. Items were retained if the item-to-total correlation was .35 or greater. Thirty-two items, eight items per scale, were retained. One item, "record my feelings in a learning journal," was retained even though the item-to-total correlation was only .25, because the work of Daudelin (1994) demonstrates the power of reflection and journaling as a learning tactic. It was also reasoned that the survey was meant for use as a pedagogical tool, and it seemed more important to introduce the concept of reflection and journaling in the classroom than to improve internal consistency of the scale.

All of the scales met an acceptable level of internal consistency of .70 or greater (Nunnally, 1978) using Cronbach's alpha, a statistic that indicates the degree to which all of the items measure the same topic or construct. Scale intercorrelations (the extent to which the items on each scale overlap the items on another scale), means, standard deviations, and medians are shown in Table 2. So, for example, about 23 percent (.48 squared) of the people who respond to *Feeling* in a certain way are likely to respond to *Accessing Others* in a similar way. On the other hand, respondents only had a 3 percent (.18 squared) tendency to respond to *Action* and *Accessing Others* in the same way. If scale intercorrelations were higher than the alpha for any dimension (shown in bold), it would mean that the scales were really measuring the same construct and not two different constructs.

Construct Validity

Construct validity refers to the relationship between the four scales of the LTI and the extent to which the use of these learning tactics is related to other measures of learning skill.

Two studies of the construct validity of the instrument were conducted. In the first study, self-report data was gathered on the LTI and on three of the scales from *Prospector*, an instrument with scales designed to measure ability and willingness to learn from experience (McCall, Schweitzer, & Mahoney, 1996). The Prospector scales used were "seeks opportunities to learn," "seeks and uses feedback," and "learns from mistakes." Alpha coefficients for these scales, as reported in the test manual, are .88, .82, and .83, respectively. In the second study, self-report ratings were collected on the LTI and boss ratings were collected on the Prospector learning scales. In both studies the participants understood that this was a research study and that their individual data would be confidential.

The results of the first study, a group of army captains who took both instruments as part of an off-site training program, are depicted in Table 3. The table shows the zero order correlations for each of the learning tactics with each of the learning scales (the criterion measures), a simple illustration of the relationship of each tactic with each learning scale. The Multiple R and R-squared for all four tactics regressed on each of the learning scales. The beta coefficients are also depicted. The Multiple R illustrates the relationship of all four tactics to each *Prospector* learning scale. The R-squared illustrates how much variance in the tactic is accounted for by the combination of all four tactics. The beta coefficient illustrates the unique variance accounted for by each tactic. In other words, the tactics are to some extent intercorrelated, and this is reflected in the zero order correlation and the Multiple R. The beta weight removes the influence of the intercorrelation of one tactic with the others and shows the relationship of each tactic with each criterion measure on the *Prospector* learning scale. Finally, the table illustrates the zero order correlation for each tactic with a Variety Index measure, a score computed for each participant by adding up how many tactics

Scale intercorrelations, alpha coefficients, means, standard deviations, and median scores for Learning Tactics Inventory (n = 274). Alphas are bold in the diagonals.

	Action	Thinking	Feeling	Accessing Others
Action	**.73**			
Thinking	.38	**.76**		
Feeling	.23	.42	**.80**	
Accessing Others	.18	.48	.48	**.76**
Mean	29.24	29.43	24.32	27.70
Standard Deviations	4.26	4.74	5.45	4.74
Median	30	30	24	28

Note: An exploratory factor analysis revealed that the scales are not unidimensional. The decision was made to maintain the four conceptual scales for ease of pedagogical use.

Table 2. Intercorrelation of Scale Items, Means, Standard Deviations, and Medians

he or she reported using that are above the median for the sample. Scores could range from 0 to 4.

The results of the second study, from a civilian population attending a corporate university leadership program, are illustrated in Table 4, which depicts the zero order correlations between the self-reported use of each of the four tactics and the Variety Index measure with boss ratings of learning behaviors. Because of the small size of the sample, it was not possible to partial out the unique variance of each tactic with the learning scales for this sample.

In both studies there is a modest relationship between the learning tactics and the criterion measure. In the self-only study with the military sample, the amount of variance accounted for by the Multiple R and the Variety measures is somewhat greater than the amount of variance accounted for by the unique contribution of each tactic. Additionally, looking at the self-only study, the use of all three criterion learning behaviors represents a unique contribution for different tactics. In other words, to be an effective learner, using all of

LTI-Prospector learning scales
Zero order, partial (beta), and multiple R Correlations
Military sample (n = 274)

Criterion Measure	Action	Thinking	Feeling	Accessing Others	R	R2	Variety
Learns from Mistakes	.13	.24** (.18)	.23** (.19)	.10	.29	.08	.26**
Seeks Opportunities to Learn	.27** (.18)	.28	.28** (.16)	.22**	.38	.14	.36**
Seeks/Uses Feedback	.18**	.30** (.18)	.23**	.29** (.17)	.36	.13	.32**
Mean	29.24	29.43	24.32	27.70			2.0
Standard Deviations	4.26	4.74	5.45	4.74			
Median	30	30	24	28			

Notes: *Correlation is significant at the .05 level. **Correlation is significant at the .01 level.
Significant partial correlations (beta coefficients) indicating unique variance are in parentheses.

Table 3. Relationship Between LTI Tactics and Prospector Learning Scales in Military Study

the learning behaviors would coincide with the need to use all of the tactics. In the second study, the Variety measure does not account for more of the variance than the use of the *Thinking* or the *Action* tactics. Sample size precluded additional investigation of these relationships.

Relationship to Meta-Cognition

Implicit in the theory proposed by Lombardo, Bunker, and Webb (1990) is that increasing one's repertoire of learning tactics is a meta-cognitive activity. However, it was not clear from this work whether meta-cognitive ability was construed as an attribute independent of the four learning sets of tactics or if meta-cognitive ability was conceptualized as one of the tactics. Using a twenty-nine item modification of a scale of meta-cognitive ability developed by Schraw and Dennison (1994), where alpha = .91, scores on the four learning

Boss/self correlations between Prospector learning scales and the Learning Tactics Inventory for a civilian population (n = 36).

Criterion Measure	Action	Thinking	Feeling	Accessing Others	Variety
Seeks Opportunities	.39*	.39*	.17**	.09	.367*
Seeks/Uses Feedback	.31	.37*	.29	.23	.406*
Learns From Mistakes	.34*	.34*	.17	.26	.301
Mean	28.25	27.92	23.17	27.58	2.25
Standard Deviations	3.52	3.83	4.26	3.95	1.38
Median	28	28	23.50	28	2.50

Notes: *Correlation is significant at the .05 level.

Table 4. Relationship Between LTI Tactics and Prospector Learning Scales in Civilian Study

tactics were correlated with the meta-cognjtive scale. Meta-cognition was correlated with the thinking tactics (r. 55,n = 26,p.> 001) and was not specifically correlated with any of the other tactics. Thus, it would appear at this stage that meta-cognition lies within the domain of the *Thinking* tactic.

Relationship to Personality

Another hypothesis imbedded in the work of Lombardo, Bunker, and Webb (1990) is that to engage in challenging and novel experiences using learning tactics appropriate to the task—rather than tactics that are habitual—requires an individual to "go against the grain" of his or her emotional and psychological comfort level. This is a critical concept because many of the popular surveys and tests measuring personality preferences, interests, and learning style speak of learning through assimilation and prescribe moving toward those activities most in keeping with one's values, style, or preferences. There has also been a move within the education field encouraging teachers to teach in a manner congruent with each student's preferred learning style or preference. However, the acquisition of knowledge in a classroom setting—even if it is kinesthetic rather than auditory or tactile—is different from the learning that occurs through mastering the challenge of a novel experience.

The *Learning Tactics Inventory* follows other research that seeks to understand and facilitate the kind of critical learning and development that takes place when individuals engage in what Seibert (1994) calls "attraction anxiety." This phrase was coined to describe how a person can be simultaneously attracted to a new and challenging opportunity while being fearful that he or she will not succeed. The LTI is meant to support learning by accommodation, as expressed in the work of Jung (1971) as well as by theorists in the realm of adult development, such as Kegan (1982) and Mezirow (1990). In their work, it is recognized that development, particularly in middle age, occurs through the mastery of challenges that are new or unfamiliar, by employing the "undeveloped" parts of one's self. Jung, for example, speaks of mid-life as the time when a person develops his or her shadow side. Adult development theorists speak of experiences that are additive versus activities and events that move an individual to experience the world differently, to create new meaning structures (Palus & Drath, 1995). Kolb (1984) describes it as "when an individual gains a new perspective, attitude, or skill because of her or his engagement in novel experience."

To the extent that learning management and leadership skills in the workplace is construed as a task of mid-life or mid-career, this learning requires an individual to engage in tasks not previously mastered and certainly not learned in school. If the approach and mastery of these tasks does not "come naturally" to an individual, this learning can be described as "going against the grain."

To test the extent to which the scales on the learning tactics represent underlying traits, preferences, or "grain"; the learning tactics were correlated with the eight scales on the *Myers-Briggs Type Indicator*: *Extroversion, Introversion, Thinking, Feeling, Sensing, Intuition, Judging,* and *Perceiving*. Before discussing the results, it is important to understand the differences between the *Myers-Briggs Type Indicator* and the *Learning Tactics Inventory*.

The *Myers-Briggs Type Indicator* and the LTI both have scales labeled *Thinking* and *Feeling*, but these labels do not mean the same thing for the two instruments. In the *Myers-Briggs Type Indicator,* the *Thinking* and *Feeling* scales are presented as opposing points of view. The theory holds that individuals who make decisions using the *Thinking* preference call on their sense of fairness and logic (true versus false), whereas individuals who use the *Feeling* preference call on their values (right versus wrong). In the LTI, the term *Thinking* refers to learning behaviors associated with solitary, internal, and cognitive processes. The term *Feeling* refers to learning behaviors having to do with recognizing and managing one's own feelings of uncertainty as well as those same feelings in others.

Remembering these differences in language, the results of this analysis are depicted in Table 5. The

Correlations of scores on the *Learning Tactics Inventory* with the personality preferences depicted by the MBTI for a military sample (n = 86).

	Action	Thinking	Feeling	Accessing
Extroversion	.08	.01	-.04	.24*
Introversion	-.10	-.02	.05	-.22*
Sensing	-.14	-.006	.10	.14
INtuition	.10	-.05	-.12	-.10
Thinking	.24*	.12	-.24*	-.11
Feeling	-.25*	-.15	-.24*	.11
Judging	-.02	.17	.08	.11
Perceiving	.04	-.19	-.06	-10

Notes: *Correlation is significant at the .05 level.

Table 5. Correlations Between MBTI and LTI for Military Sample

significant correlations between the Myers Briggs scales and the LTI scales are between *Accessing Others* from the LTI and the *Extrovert* from the MBTI and between *Action* (LTI) and the MBTI *Feelings* scale. As Table 5 illustrates, to employ the tactics that form the scale *Accessing Others* would to some extent require "Introverts" to go against the grain. To employ tactics that fall under the heading labeled *Action* would require individuals with an MBTI *Feelings* preference to go against the grain. To illustrate the point, the LTI *Action* scale includes items such as "moving ahead despite resistance from others." This behavior would be much less compatible with an individual with MBTI *Feeling* preferences, who would not necessarily move ahead despite resistance from others but would very much want to take into account the feelings of others. The MBTI F might well value affiliation and harmony over and above getting something done in a timely manner. The versatile learner would be able to take action when it was necessary, even though it might require him or her to go against the grain.

Concurrent Validity: Relationship to Managerial Effectiveness

Concurrent validity refers to the relationship between the four scales of the LTI and measures of managerial effectiveness at a given point in time.

Implicit in the use of a variety of learning tactics to achieve one's developmental goals is the hypothesis that individuals who are better learners are, or will become, better managers. Three studies were conducted to explore this hypothesis.

The first study was conducted with the military sample previously described. Self-report ratings on the LTI scales were correlated with self-report ratings on the end-state competencies scales of the *Prospector* instrument. These end-state competency scales are designed to measure the skills apparent in effective and experienced managers (McCall, Spreitzer, & Mahoney, 1996). These scales are labeled "Is Insightful," "Is Committed to Making a Difference;" "Has the Courage to Take Risks," "Seeks Broad Business Knowledge," "Acts with Integrity," "Adapts to Cultural Differences," and "Brings Out the Best in People." Alphas for the criterion measures as described in the manual range from .79 to .89.

Data for the second study were collected from the previously described corporate university sample using self-report ratings on the LTI and boss ratings on the *Prospector* end-state competency scales.

For the third study we used a different criterion measure of effectiveness sixteen items from the multi-source feedback instrument, *Benchmarks* (Lombardo & McCauley, 1988). *Benchmarks* is an instrument designed to measure lessons learned from experience. Section 3 of this instrument contains sixteen items describing various managerial assignments, for example, "being promoted into an unfamiliar line of business," "having a significant role in an acquisition," "being promoted two or more levels," and so forth. (See Figure 3 for a list of items.) Raters (bosses, peers, and subordinates of the target manager) are asked to respond to each item by answering the following question: "How effectively would this person handle each of the following jobs?" and to respond using one of the following anchors: "among the worst," "less well than most," "adequately," "better than most," "among the best." The alpha for these sixteen items totaled together and used as a proxy measure for current or potential managerial effectiveness was .93.

The participants in the third study were 188 individuals from a number of different organizations attending a leadership development program at a not-for-profit research and education center.

Tables 6, 7, and 8 illustrate the results of these three studies. Table 6 depicts the zero order correlations between each of the tactics and the Variety measure and the self-ratings of managerial effectiveness. Also depicted are the results of the Multiple R and the unique contribution (beta coefficients) of each of the tactics to the regression equation. As opposed to the relationship of the tactics to the learning scales, the amount of variance accounted for by the Multiple R or the Variety measure is not greater than the amount of variance accounted for by the unique contribution of a single tactic and the use of the *Accessing Others* tactic is not significantly related to any of effectiveness measures. In fact, *Accessing Others* is negatively

Criterion measures for concurrent validity study of managerial effectiveness taken from the Benchmarks® Instrument.

1. Turning around an organization or unit in trouble when he or she has full authority to do so.
2. Starting something from scratch.
3. Turning around an organization or unit in trouble when he or she has insufficient formal authority to make people comply.
4. Working more than six months in a foreign country.
5. Being promoted into an unfamiliar line of business.
6. Switching from a line job to a staff job.
7. Changing to much more responsibility (more people, functions, and money).
8. Having a significant role in an acquisition.
9. Having six months to close down an operation.
10. Negotiating a major contract.
11. Installing a new system on a project basis when the installation is resisted.
12. Serving on a task force to solve a major problem.
13. Moving laterally into an unfamiliar line of business (no promotion).
14. Being promoted in the same function or division (moving a level up).
15. Switching from a staff job to a line job.
16. Being promoted two or more levels.

Figure 3. Criterion Measures for *Benchmarks* Instrument

related to one's self-perception of "Insightful," someone described as bright and quick, with new approaches to issues.

Table 7 depicts the boss scores on the effectiveness measures compared to the self-ratings on tactics and illustrates that only the self-reported use of the *Thinking* tactic is related to any of the boss-rated criterion measures.

Table 8 depicts the zero order correlations between each of the tactics and the assignment potential criterion measure as rated by the self, boss, peers, and direct reports. (Zero order correlations for each of the relationships for each of the rater groups are available from the author.) In this case, tactics are illustrated when p. = or < .05 but words are used rather than the correlation coefficients to provide a better picture of relationships

LTI-Prospector end-state competency scales (military sample, n = 274)

	Action	Thinking	Feeling	Accessing Others	R	R2	Variety
Acts with Integrity	.09	.27** (.25)	.20**	.12*	.29	.08	.24**
Broad Business Knowledge	.26** (.22)	.21** (.20)	.03	.00	.31	.10	.12
Best in People	.23** (.15)	.26** (.20)	.18**	.13**	.31	.09	.24**
Committed to Making a Difference	.27** (.20)	.26** (.20)	.11	.12	.32	.11	.26**
Courage to Take Risks	.33** (.30)	.21**	.09	.07	.34	.12	.20**
Insightful	.23** (.15)	.25** (.21)	.16*	.02(-.15)	.32	.10	.23**
Adapts to Cultural Differences	.13*	.14*	.23** (.16)	.19**	.26	.07	.22*

Notes: *Correlation is significant at the .05 level. **Correlation is significant at the .01 level. Significant partial correlations (beta coefficients) indicating unique variance are in parentheses.

Table 3. Relationship Between Self-Reported Effectiveness and Use of Learning Tactics

across rater groups. In this analysis, it is interesting to note that the Variety measure was only significant with ratings made by the peer and self rater groups; that *Feelings* was significantly related to only one of the potential assign ments from the direct report perspective; and that *Accessing Others* was negatively related (except from the self point of view) to various criterion measures of managerial effectiveness.

Conclusions and Limits of the Research

The four scales on the *Learning Tactics Inventory* demonstrate fair to good internal consistency, sufficient for

LTI-Prospector end-state competency scales (self/boss sample, n = 36).

	Action	Thinking	Feeling	Accessing Others	Variety
Acts with Integrity	-.26	.09	-.09	.14	-.008
Broad Business. Knowledge	-.16	-.12	-.13	-.02	-.08
Best in people	.06	-.12	-.13	-.02	.227
Committed to Making a Difference	.15	.33*	.05	.06	.251
Courage to Take Risks	.25	.22	.10	.15	.265
Insightful	-.05	.10	.24	.21	.076
Adapts to Cultural Differences	.02	.33*	.11	.08	.079

Notes: *Correlation is significant at the .05 level.

Table 7. Relationship Between Boss-Reported Effectiveness and Use of Learning Tactics

pedagogical use. The construct validation studies illustrated in Tables 3 and 4 offer support for the hypothesis that individuals who can use all four tactics are more versatile learners than individuals who use one, two, or three of the tactics. The data in Table 6, which correlates boss *Prospector* data with self *Learning Tactics Inventory* data suggest that shared variance between *Prospector* end-state competencies and the *Learning Tactics Inventory* is primarily limited to the use of the *Thinking* tactics.

More data must be collected to understand whether this represents the shared variance between the instruments or the valued behaviors and culture of a particular organization. It may be that in some

Measure	Direct Reports (n = 168)	Peers (n = 182)	Boss (n = 147)	Self (n = 188)
Turn Around: Full Authority	Action, Thinking	Thinking, Variety		Action, Thinking, Variety
Scratch	-Accessing		Action	Action, Thinking, Variety
Turn Around: Insufficient Authority	Action, Thinking, Feeling			Action, Thinking, Variety
Foreign Assignment			Action	
Promoted into Unfamiliar Line of Business	-Accessing			
Line to Staff				
Huge Leap	Thinking	Variety		Action, Thinking, Variety
Significant Acquisition Role	Action, -Accessing			Action, Thinking
Close Down Operation	Action, Thinking			Action
Major Contract Negotiation	Thinking	Thinking	-Accessing	Action
Install New System Resisted	Thinking			
Major Task Force				Action, Thinking, Variety
Lateral Move Unfamiliar Line of Business				
Promoted One Level Same Function, Division				Action, Variety
Staff to Line		Variety		Action
Promoted Two or More Levels	Thinking			Action, Variety
Potential	Action, Thinking			Action, Variety

Table 8. Four Perspectives on Learning Tactics and Managerial Potential

organizations only certain tactics are considered valuable and appropriate. This could suggest that skills best mastered through the missing tactics will not be present in an organization.

Table 8 illustrates the complexity of the construct of "effectiveness" and perhaps illustrates that, in the United States, when managerial effectiveness is rated by bosses, it is still framed through the template of the action-oriented and intelligent individual achiever. Ratings and relationships from the point of view of the self, the direct reports, and the peers point to a richer view of effectiveness and the relationship with a variety of learning tactics. However, the negative relationship of *Accessing Others* with various criterion measures points to the danger of overusing a tactic and, in this case, being seen as dependent or "unable to stand on your own two feet."

Appendix A: Suggested Resources

Center for Creative Leadership. (2015). *Benchmarks® for Learning Agility™*. Greensboro, NC: Author.

Center for Creative Leadership. (2015). *Benchmarks® for Managers™*. Greensboro, NC: Author.

Center for Creative Leadership. (2014). *Experience Explorer™*. Greensboro, NC: Author.

Bunker, K. A. & Webb, A. D. (1992). *Learning how to learn from experience: Impact of stress and coping.* Greensboro, NC: Center for Creative Leadership.

Dalton, M. (1998). *Becoming a More Versatile Learner.* Greensboro, NC: Center for Creative Leadership.

Experience Explorer™. (2014). Greensboro, NC: Center for Creative Leadership.

Hallenbeck, G. (2016). *Learning agility: Unlock the lessons of experience.* Greensboro, NC: Center for Creative Leadership.

Lombardo, M.M., & McCauley, C. (1988). *Benchmarks.* Greensboro, NC: Center for Creative Leadership.

McCall, M.W., Jr., Spreitzer, G., & Mahoney, J. (1996). *Prospector.* Greensboro, NC: Center for Creative Leadership.

McCall, M.W., Jr., Lombardo, M.M., & Morrison, A.M. (1988). *The lessons of experience: How successful executives develop on the job.* Lexington, MA: Lexington Books.

McCauley, C. D. (2006). *Developmental assignments: Creating learning experiences without changing jobs.* Greensboro, NC: Center for Creative Leadership.

McCauley, C.D., DeRue, D.S., Yost, P.R., and Taylor, S. (2014). *Experience-driven leader development: Models, tools, best practices, and advice for on-the-job development.* San Francisco, CA: John Wiley and Sons.

McCauley, C. D., & McCall, M. W., Jr. (Eds.). (2014). *Using experience to develop leadership talent: How organizations leverage on-the-job development.* San Francisco: John Wiley & Sons.

Ruderman, M.N., & Ohlott, P.J. (2000). *Learning from life: Turning life's lessons of experience into leadership experience*. Greensboro, NC: Center for Creative Leadership.

Wick, C.W, & Leon, L.S. (1993). *The learning edge: How smart managers and smart companies stay ahead.* New York: McGraw-Hill.

Appendix B: Presentation Slides

LEARNING TACTICS INVENTORY

Center for
Creative
Leadership

Copyright © 2016 Center for Creative Leadership.

Slide 1

RESEARCH QUESTION

When you think about your career as a manager, certain events or episodes probably stand out in your mind—things that led to a lasting change in you as a manager. Please identify 3 key events in your career, things that made a difference in the way you manage now.

• What happened?

• What did you learn from it (for better or worse)?

Copyright © 2016 Center for Creative Leadership.

Slide 2

THE VARIETY OF EXPERIENCE

Challenging Assignments	Learning from Others	Hardships	Other Events
• Cultural Crossing	• Bosses & Superiors	• Career Setback	• Coursework & Training
• Horizontal Move	• Difficult People	• Crisis	• Personal Experience
• Increase in Job Scope	• Feedback & Coaching	• Ethical Dilemma	
• New Initiative		• Mistake	
• Stakeholder Engagement			
• Turnaround/ Fix-It			

Slide 3

LEARNING TACTICS

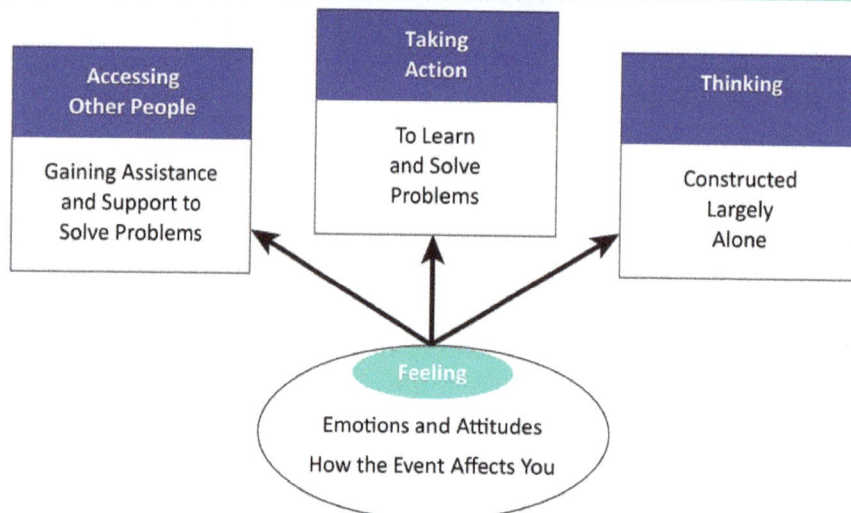

Accessing Other People
Gaining Assistance and Support to Solve Problems

Taking Action
To Learn and Solve Problems

Thinking
Constructed Largely Alone

Feeling
Emotions and Attitudes
How the Event Affects You

Slide 4

Slide 5

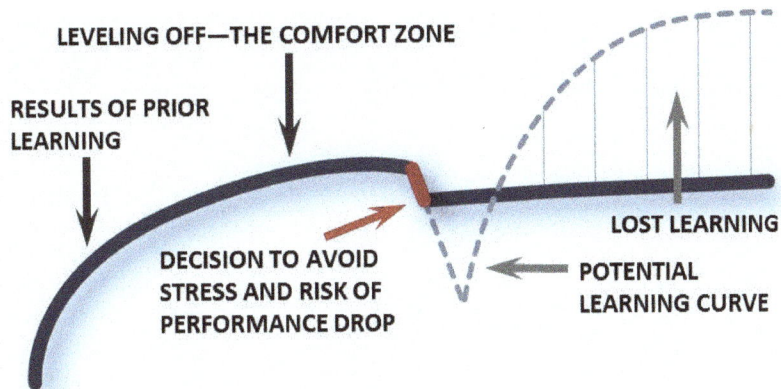

AVOIDING A LEARNING EXPERIENCE

LEVELING OFF—THE COMFORT ZONE

RESULTS OF PRIOR LEARNING

DECISION TO AVOID STRESS AND RISK OF PERFORMANCE DROP

LOST LEARNING

POTENTIAL LEARNING CURVE

Slide 6

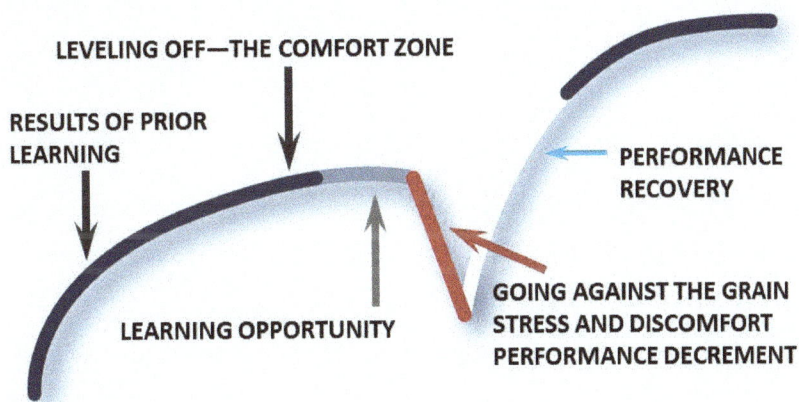

ACCEPTING THE CHALLENGE

LEVELING OFF—THE COMFORT ZONE

RESULTS OF PRIOR LEARNING

PERFORMANCE RECOVERY

LEARNING OPPORTUNITY

GOING AGAINST THE GRAIN STRESS AND DISCOMFORT PERFORMANCE DECREMENT

KEYS TO LEARNING FROM EXPERIENCE

- Awareness of what you don't do well at all

- Selecting uncomfortable learning projects

- Trying new tactics

Slide 7

Center for Creative Leadership®

About the Center for Creative Leadership

The Center for Creative Leadership (CCL®) is a top-ranked, global provider of leadership development. By leveraging the power of leadership to drive results that matter most to clients, CCL transforms individual leaders, teams, organizations and society. Our array of cutting-edge solutions is steeped in extensive research and experience gained from working with hundreds of thousands of leaders at all levels. Ranked among the world's Top 5 providers of executive education by *Financial Times* and in the Top 10 by *Bloomberg BusinessWeek*, CCL has offices in Greensboro, NC; Colorado Springs, CO; San Diego, CA; Brussels, Belgium; Moscow, Russia; Addis Ababa, Ethiopia; Johannesburg, South Africa; Singapore; Gurgaon, India; and Shanghai, China.

TOP 5 2016 FINANCIAL TIMES WORLDWIDE EXECUTIVE EDUCATION

www.ingramcontent.com/pod-product-compliance
Lightning Source LLC
Chambersburg PA
CBHW050040220326

41599CB00044B/7236